Planet Imagination (JCN's Video, Music, and Story Publishing).

Rap Stories

Author's Biography and Commentary

My name is Jamarcus Cordel Newton. I am 24years old and I am from Montgomery Alabama. I enjoy trying new things, meeting new people and going new places. I take pride in everything I do and I manage to have fun where ever I go. I am very thankful for the people God put in my life. I have an associate degree in (CIS) Computer Information System that I receive from Trenholm State Technical College. I am currently enroll at Alabama State University working on a bachelor's degree in communication. Like so many other youth in my generation I wanted to be rapper. I found passion in my music. It was a way for me to express myself. Most importantly it gave me something possible to do with my free time. Everyone needs a passion and a hobby. I have always consider music more of a hobby than a career because I knew the lack of possible to making it in the industry. Lack of role models, limited experiences and resources have cause many youth to pursue a career in music industry. A business that has so little opportunity for new talent. Many youth also pursue a career in music because they feel that it is a quick way to earn money fast. I would never tell anyone to not follow theirs dreams. People can accomplish anything they put their mind too. However the music business has both a possible and negative outcome in the world. Because of difficulty of the music industry I decided to take a different path. This book contains random lyrics that I have written over the years. I will always have a passion for music weather I am recording, writing, or just listening. *Biography written and last update, May 25,2012*

Rap Stories

Some people

() Some people talk the talk but can't walk the walk but I don't just don't talk the talk. I walk the walk. That don't mean that you shouldn't pay attention when I'm specking especially when I get to rapping then I just start clicking. I don't just be rapping I be teaching. I don't just be rapping I be preaching. So you might just learn something if you pay attention, shut up and listen. Get me heat like baked chicken. I read in a book that "wisdom is not like money to be tied up and hidden." So let me stated my opinion like Martin Luther King because both of us had a dream. Be trying to make up a scheme will I sleep in the middle of the night. Stay ready to fight. I will never bag back and bag down. What you mean that my bark is worst my bit? Physic. Tried to hard to get here. Now that I'm here. I will not be move just like Rose Parks. Ball down my pinky and ball down my thumb. Hold up three fingers in the middle and be like read between the lines. If you still don't understand then let me explain to you what it is I'm saying. Stand up very brave and start marching like a parade. Out up yo mouth and being to say. "ain't going to let nobody turn me around, turn me round, turn me round. I'm going to kept walking, kept on marching. Marching to the freedom land." Planet Imagination

That's my girl. Don't act surprise

() Hey man just don't act surprise looking at me with then big old eyes. You know my girl can slip and slide like Trina who be ready to ride like bonnie and clyde. Its us against the world. I like the way her body twirl I like the way her body whirl. Drink water start to dance probably make it rain. Foxy like Vivica sexy as Lil Kim. Them other girls hating on you but baby fuck them. Step in the game and put all these other ladies to shame. Its so insane. Not any girl in here finna take your fame. Now lets have some fun. Time for me to stray up but I ain't talking about no gun. Let me put on my rubber before I releases sperm get inside yo body wiggle like worms. Multiple like germs beat it hard than a drum until your body get num do it like the rice crispy treat box make it snap crackle pop. Drop on it like a raindrop and make you do the bunny hop.

Brand new trend
()Spinning off juice and gin start a brand new trend by breaking other niggas girlfriends in. They a 10 out of 10 and I'm popular like sin plus I flow like the wind. Do you really wanna battle you ain't never going to win. Which means you dudes going to lose now you sadder than the blues. Bluer than Gonzo. I got a crush on Miranda Cosgrove. 45 on my waist it will blow you to outer space and send you straight to the cosmos. In space nobody can hear you scream. So fresh so clean with a kill team. Red shot laser beam knock out yo spline. Now you walking like you bowing. Pull up to the club all the girls get to shouting. Everybody hear them screaming. So freak so clean sipping on that blue hurricane. That drinks in my system. It made horny now she feel it in her spine. Next night having wet dreams it's the moment of my season and I'm living my dreams and ain't no hater in here finna block my swag.

She always classy
() She always classy she never trashy. Come home like lassie. You can come to my home and we can play house. She can nibble on my bone suck on it like a ice cream cone. I know you wanna lick the rapper. I know you taste the flavor. Sweeter than now and laters. If need loving you can get it now and later. Do it right now and can do it later but not on the same day may I'm going to call you tomorrow or it maybe tonight. Every day out of 7 we talk on the phone from 8:00 to 11:00. When I'm with you feels like I got a piece of heaven. My ebony goddess, my Nubian queen. You so fine make an angel want to fall in love. Skin so soft, like feathers from a dove. From the first time I saw you, I knew it had to be love. Thought I was a player, and had the game on lock. I gave it all up, when I final met you my forever valentine my pretty black fox. Unique from the rest of the flock.

I Know we in American
() I Know we in American with the bill of rights and the 1st Amendment is the freedom of speech but before you get to talking all stuff that you be talking and you think it's going to be alright. Un-uh, not really. Better wise up you and think again silly cause don't know weak people walk around in the streets of the Gump city. Don't stop at no hick town where you can pick to hit likely split. Profession pimps, real gangsters no wangster . Better listen to yo parents when they tells not to talk to strangers. My white friends turned green like Tommy from power rangers. collect mo white than snow angles. Flyer than an angel and on fire like a demon. Holy water planned, plotting and scheming. With a plan or plot to tried to try to make it to the stop. As you can tell this is not Kenan and Kel. On a whole other level. Serious like sickle cell. And I wouldn't stay in the middle because I wouldn't get caught plus I ain't doing nothing illegal I'm going to rise to the top.

Take over the world
() Take over the world and put it in my pocket. Lock it up like the pictures inside of a locket. Eat it up like a homeless person who found a brand new pack of bologna. Everybody who believes in Jesus should have their own personal testimony. So everybody who is anybody that has ever had problems. It's time to spread the word to put Jesus first. The word of God is free to everybody it should not be kept be a secret like what's inside a woman's purse. Time and time again we all want to lie just to try to make it by. My advice is get down on your knees and pray. Maybe tomorrow will be a brighter day. You might not have a lot but just don't lose faith. That will be a big mistake. God got something better in store but in the meantime I'm kept on going singing sing this lil light of mine. It might not be here when I want it but it will be here right on time. Plus I read in the book of Ephesians a couple of reasons that would make me believe that every thing happens for a reason. So I'm just going to chill and wait for my season.

Bedroom Boom

() Meet me in the living room so we can do the bedroom boom. Got me floating on cloud 9. It's like I'm walking on the moon. Banging like drums make yo body go num. make you moan. make you groan. make you cum. Why you acting so nervous baby we is both grown just turned 19 with a body like lighting that drive me wild like a Viking. Her kisses taste like icing. It taste so delightful I wanted her wifey. She my queen and her Caesars. Shopping spread visa. I promise to love you for ever right hand on the bible.

Human Development

() Let's talk about human development and character traits. Knows body perfect. Everybody makes mistakes. Just like Hannah Montana say. Sometime I fell tupac. Its me against the world. Nobody understands how I fell. I want cry out a tear. Smile on the outside but live my life with so much fear. The only I true express my self is though the music. The sound of the rhyme and groove and movement. I swear if it wasn't for rapping I would lose it. That's way I praying for a recorder deal but let me go ahead and kill the stereotype. Ever rapper is not trying to sell dope. Gangbang get shot with the pistol cock while trying to promote sex. So if you see me in yo neighborhood. It's ok relax. Because I already know that I'm be in chill mood. Cause God walking with me who going to come against me. As I walk through the valley of the shadow of death moving through the darkest looking for the wealth. But its still not worth my health. Get rich or die trying is not my Lords will. I perfect to be broke and living, cause as long as I'm alive I bet you that I'm rich in holy though which means I can do anything.

Don't be hating on my girl.

() Man don't be hating on my girl. Don't be tripping on girl. She shine, she a pearl. I'll give her the world. I'll do good deeds for her like my name was Earl. Show you a whole new world like Aladdin did Jasmine. Go to work every morning so I can bring home the bacon. That way you can get what ever you need it in whole no fractions. Freak you on the couch or freak you on the mattress. Put you to bed now you feeling relaxation. Floating on cloud 9. My forever valentine. I wanna do it from the front, from the side, from behind. You far a dime. You a dollar plus 99. I'm be here for you until the end of time.

Kids Need Hugs

() Kids need hugs not drugs but these drugs got me carrots than Bugs. On the corner with a white glove and a black glove. Fake niggas hate and real niggas show love. What it is what it was. Hype like them niggas in the clubs. Drunk on that buzz bottle fill with suzy. Everybody who is anybody get lose off that crunk juice. I stay hustling trying to my paper stick out like the belly of Bruce Bruce. Are you talking bout that niggia from comic view. Hell yeah. What the fuck going to do. You want make some bout it. Better back the fuck up off of me before you get you freaking tooth knock lose. Somebody please call the tooth fairy. I'm well supply like the military. Leave you smocking like Jim Carrey. Found missing on the 5:00 news say hello to Tanya Terry. I suggest you find sanctuary. Lock down nun you don't really none. So just move to yo happy place and if I was you I wouldn't come back out to play for the rest of the day.

Lil mama super sonic

() Lil mama super sonic. And lil mama so exotic. Lil mama body rocking. We doing it none stopping. Pop, lock and dropping. Lil mama so neurotic drop on it like hydraulics. Long hair, light skin, she look like Pocahontas. I make you cry like onions. She got them tears of joy. Licking on yo body and it taste like chips ahoy. Plus I'm yo love boy toy and you my love girl doll. We can do it all. From the window to the wall. From the ceiling to the floor. Let's hit the mall and ball. Start off small now you got it hard now and my dick standing tall. Strength out like a log. Put it down yo throat now you talking like a frog.

I read in book
() I read in a book by Joel Osteen page 19 "You can not soar with eagles if you keep pecking chickens." Plus a saint is just a sinner who ran out of luck fell down and got they ass right back up. So when ever life gives you hurtles just leaping over them like ninja turtles. Sometimes yo feelings get hurt like a mad lady giving birth. Having the child of a no good baby daddy. But Jesus is on yo side they ain't even on yo level. You golfer and they caddy. Every who believes in love and kiss and hug and never do drugs because they got that natural hi. They looking at you funny. yo kinfolks and friends is wondering why. Just look em straight in eye and tell'em. "This joy that I have the world didn't give it and the world can't take it a way." Even though sometimes life might get hard. Get toss around and shuffle like a deck of cards. Step on like carpets seem like the Devil got you aim and lock like a target. 1. 2. 3. The Devil throwing stinks fell like he hit upside my head with brick. That's O.K. Let me find my click and crew. We through like Ray Charles and make it do what it got to. And don't be looking at me all mean eyes. You must not have read Philippians 4:13. "I can do all things through Christ who strengths me." So everybody needs to step up and stop lame. Get some confidence. God did not give us the spirit of fear. So why you wanna cry out a tear. Suggest you strapped up. Get ready just like Madea would. Just like we all should.

Nobody going to touch me.
() God walking me. Nobody going to touch me. My cup over flowing. Watch me switch game over. Paper stacking up bigger than Paul Bunyan. Make these rappers cry like onions. On the sideline complaining. Like how he do that. Cause I'm bad, cause I'm gutta, case I'm raw, case I'm smooth. Because I'm saved. So don't play me like a arcade. Serious like aids. Go ahead and hit highway. Get away like a slave. Moving like Forrest Gump. Run rapper, run rapper. Smooth boy get me got that tongue twister flow that'll twist up like braids. Don't make me release my rage, like a tiger out the cage, hit you like Johnny Cage. Don't ever act my age. The faith of a child, the soul of a old man and energy of a teenager. Now I gotta lay you suckers like a my space page. God Dam! I'm pay. So much. money, money. So much money, money. If I buy something else I still have money, money. And I got so many girls, girls. so many girls, girls. If you took half I'll still have more. And I do this everyday. like every single day. Monday, Tuesday, Wednesday Thursday Friday Saturday Sunday. Like on Monday, Tuesday, Wednesday Thursday Friday Saturday Sunday.

<u>As I step out the shower</u>
() As I step out the shower, my heart starts to race, thinking about all the many places on your body that I could taste. As I look at your face and stare into yo eyes then I gaze at you soul and the love inside stacks up like hay. Messaging on your shoulders like clay. Rubbing down your arms, would you be my magic charm. The sunshine in my thunderstorm. My price in a box of cereal. The prettiest picture in the mirror. The colors in my rainbow. The sweetest in my honey and the value in my money. I'm trying to get at you like a star in the sky I might not reach but I can't help but try. Cause you so fine and I want you to be mine, so we exchange kisses over wine. I want you to be my forever valentine. If your love was falling leaves, then I am the rake. You the pretties girl in the Untied States. Stink it from behind make you feel in you vertebrate. I know felt the Earth shake. Hold you close so you can't escape. If I don't get with it will be the world's biggest mistake.

<u>These niggas bullshitting</u>
() These niggas bullshitting. Man you got alot to say and you talk alot stuff. I think you mouth need some sanitary. I'm well supplied like the military. I suggest you find sanctuary. My rhymes is extraordinary. Way above ordinarily. Outrageous vocabulary.

Put the beat in a cemetery. Somebody stop me I'm smock Jim Carrey. Sparkle like the Tinkerbell fairy. Your girl wanted to seduce me but her pussy was hairy. So I beat her cousin instead. She licking on my abs with whip cream and strawberries. Now she talking about marriage. Got me feeling kinda scary. She wanna be Mariah Carey and she want me to be her Nick Cannon. So I went along with it. Stuck it in her mouth and told her she was wilding out. And as when she finished I was like I have to roll, bounce. She like baby where you going. What you don't knew. I gotta get back to money. And tell these sideline rockies to stop looking at me funny.

Stuck in the middle
() You right! I ain't from hood and I ain't never been to jail. Growing up in the country living in the suburbs. Stuck in the middle like Malcolm livening from pay check to pay check. Man I just can't take that. I'm mad like a niggia first time with a driver's license just got in a car wreck. In dept deeper than the grand crayon. Do it feel like every time you get up in the world then a niggia knock you down. But its still ok. For a saint is just a sinner who got knock down and got back up again. So I got back up and had to realize don't act surprise looking at me with them mean mugging eyes like Maya Angelo still I rise. I got nothing to lose but everything to gain and everything to prove start paying my pay tithes and start paying my and started paying my dues. While I'm out here slaving working an honest job thinking about misbehaving doing something illegal on the sideline just to get a lil extra paper. Then I had a vision I was like woow! hold up. Am I doing everything that I could be doing. Am I'm going to church paying attention. Case the Bible say give ten percent and save ten percent. But what about the rent. That's the 10%. I use for rent plus somebody hit me on the side of my car now my bumper got a dent. But trust me cuz. God will provide a long life of love if follow the bible and never drugs. If you walk with Jesus then when you make one step then he'll take two steps. Se sometimes the devil smacks you face. The world is a big place but we all Gods children. There is no supreme race. She does it just like he and he do it she does. And they do it like all the rest do. Put you middle in the finger in air and the devil he threw.

Mamma-Mia
() Mamma-Mia stop acing lame and bring out your fame. Step in the game and put all these other ladies to shame. Now it's so insane. You body picture perfect I want to beat it out frame. Get up inside of it like children inside of a tent. Won't stop until yo body get a dent. I get to blushing now I'm shining like lamp and about to catch a cramp. Be on top of it like a stamp, and you the envelope. Nice pink whatcha call it between yo legs beat it to it turn red same color as watermelon, but when I ate it taste like cantaloupe and trust me there is a difference. But when it comes to the rest of these girls in world there is no difference. All these other girls is so plain because they all the same but not you. your love is different. You unique from the rest of the sheep in the flock.

Rap Game Solution
() It's lil Jamarcus Newton and I'm the rap game solution world wide like population. Hardcore gangster rapper but I ain't got time for this foolish which means I ain't got to gun shot, pop, pop, get shot, beat you like Pootie tang, gangbang, dope slang, but I'm still

off the chain. Too insane in midbrain. Cursing in fast lane, looking for the fast cash. Best believe I'm out yo range. This here is my domain . I run this dominion stay on my own dimension. Ever caught me sipping. Plus I got goon squad full of military type menaces. Out up my mouth and spit magic like a genuine. Mo flyer than Aladdin's carpet. I got u suckers on lock and aim like a target. Look on the side line and saw Ryan writing yo life away with a sharpie. Nigga on level: hardly, barely, rarely, occasionally, sometimes, maybe. The hypes rapper rhyming is who I be each and every time. Hit me up for a track any and every time cause I got 16 bars or more that will leave you mesmerize. Plus I'm a mastermind. Fresher than pine-sol and toxic like turpentine.

If want to be somebody
() If want to be somebody and you want to go somewhere you better wake up and pay attention. Determination and motivation like TI. Can't you see I'm on a mission. As long as long as I can breathe then I'm alive so I shall will survive. But baby I'm not rich but just give me a chance to advance my status. Get the fuck up out of here, hop on that midnight train Gladys. Become a legendary pimp. Compared to me you is a imp. Now its seven o'clock (7:00) on the dot riding around in drop top. Pretend that I'm Usher so I'm going to do it my way. Become a music legend just like Marvin Gaye. All work and no play makes for a very dull day. That's why when I work I play and when I play I work. I'm always on a hustle. Be all that I can be just like army. Always strive to do my best that's the way you stay bless turn off the stress this storm is just a test start walking with Jesus and touch the sky like Kanye West. But first I need a workout plan God sent me a guardian angel to lend me a helping hand. Se someday I'm going to stand up on my own two feet and become a real man. Just like the high school band. I will always marching. Marching to the freedom land.

Kill you three ways
() Blast with pistols. Kill yo ass 3 ways like rock, paper, scissor. I make rain you make it Dr-ig-so. Stay so fresh like breath that just ate a box of altoids. I ain't made to played with like a little child with toys. So don't get all gangster all me Lil homie. You acting kinda cocky. Don't let this shit go to your head. It get all big headed and swell up like Jlo booty. Now welcome to the gump where boys pop the truck, ain't no punks hit you in yo chest and have walking with a lump. Now they look like Quasimodo. Better lay as low ho. All that bragging and boost want to show the fuck off in public but when its private time behind close doors yall turn into some ho's. vanished like ghosts. Abracadabra, hocus pocus. Its too late for all that. You got heated a thanksgiving roast. Light yo ass fire and turn you into toast. I bet next time you know better. You must have thought I was joking. Chopper hit you from side and put yo body in rotation just like we was smocking.

She all that
() She all that and a bag of hot flaming potato chips with big hips switch when she walk. Sexy lil thang that lick her lips when she talk. Long curly hair. You love her like a care bears. You can't help but too stare. Because she so fine and she shine and I wanna make her mine. Got me floating on cloud 9. My forever valentine. You far from a dime. You a dollar plus 99. I'm going be here for you until the end of time. I don't see nothing wrong with a little bump and grind from behind, from the side, from the front. When I tell you that I love you then that's not no front. I ain't gotta trick, plan, pot or deceive. Every night I thank God for your love when I get on my knees. I promise to satisfy all your needs. Mental, physical, sexual, emotional. Take a sip of a that holy water. Drink from my magic potion. It will put yo back in motion. Have you linking like a ocean.

Similar to an ant
() In the words of Paul Wall "I'm similar to an ant because I'm low to the Earth." But that's O.K. Yeah it's ok. Because Jesus ain't no stranger, ain't no stranger. He was born in a manager. Like to ride with the bottom class, like to roll with the bottom class and make them rise to the top. You know who I look up to them old ladies in church. All always got a pursue full of peppermints. I'm going to try to talk a fine one after service and let them smell the evidence, give her a kiss and let her taste the evidence. Tell'em like Steve

Hardy don't trip he ain't through with me yet. Matter of fact he ain't through with you yet. Cause we all gods children and all have stuff to learn. Everything comes in due season but you have to wait your turn. Because everybody on a high way to hell trying to make it heaven some way. I need to swear over and change lanes so I can make to heaven some day.

What we Gotta Do
() I got an oral so mean but I'm so smooth and nice. They nickname cup because I go good with ice. You seen the way I shine bling, bling. Post up on the Carbinen. Sipping Hennessey and drink like pirate. Do you really want battle you finna the start a riot. I'm gonna cut you like Jack Sparrow and cut you in stomach and make you vomit. Exploded like a bomb. Motherfucker boom. Nigga. I'm atomic. Bandage yo body and have you draped up mummy. Now I feel like Tommy. Who is that. That's the baby form Rug rats. Now nigga guess what. Now I gotta do what I gotta do like baby's gotta do what a baby's gotta do. And when I come through with me and my crew we make it do. Cause we wanna do what we wanna do. and we don't give a flying fuck about you. Why. Cause I'm pimp and you a ho you. I'm yogi bear and bobo you'll bust a cap up in my ass. Naw! But I will bust a cap up you ass and give you a bobo made hard for you dodo.

Another type of reality.
() Hold up Lil mama, let me whisper in your ear. Teel something strictly confidential only your ears can hear. I love you so much that I want to wait for marriage. But keep it totally off the record. My friends just going to laugh. They don't understand how I feel. I'm speaking on my behalf. And I don't know what I can say to make you feel better. I called you on the phone and wrote you love letters. You are the best thing that ever happened to me. When I go to sleep at night and dream, your face is the only thing I see. I want you more than anything in this life. I can't wait for the day you decide to be my wife. I wish you can tell me what's wrong, so I can make the pain go away. No matter how long it takes, my love is here to stay. Your love is the key and my heart is the lock let me open up soul and take you 2 another galaxy. Planet Imagination is a another type of reality. Where you can live everyday like a fantasy.

I wish they would
() I wish they would say that I ain't hard cause I ain't come from hood. You right. I grew up in the country. Going fish with granddad, grandmamma in kitchen cooking greens, little boy with big dream. In the middle of night while I sleep, while I dream trying to make up a scheme be smooth like ice cream. Cousins going hunting in the woods and I wish these suckers would say that I ain't hard cause I ain't came from hood. I was like in innocent nigga in jail who couldn't really afford bail. In the Doctor office screaming mommy please take away my sickle cell. No I'm living in the suburbs where the green grass always grows and the birds stay chirping just like them new phone sound like stay singing Christmas carols 24, 7 I got a step daddy name Daryl. Wish him the best and a long fill success. God bless even though we hardly ever talk. Walking with no specking but he preaching like a deacon but his son has testimony. My dreams get bigger they multiply like germs. but through life I have learn that I can not crawl and curve like worm. After let down and let down. Been in the hospital after hospital. They said it was

impossible that's when I started listening to the gospel. Now nothing is impossible.

Throwing dollars with cousins
() Throwing dollars that's why they wanna holla. Popping Pina colada. I ain't three six mafia but I stay popping my collar. Fucking with me and my cousin we showed up deep by the dozen. Fuck with me and my kin you ain't never going to win. sipping off juice and gin. Start a brand trend by breaking other peoples girlfriends in they a 10 out of 10. Isn't no need to taking to like big wolf. Cause they always let me in. I be up in that pussy. Little girl. Little girl would you let me in. Make the hairs on neck roll up to the back of yo chiny, chin, chin. Be ready to be broken in. Fuck what heard better ask my cousin bird if most of these dudes be talking but ain't never about their word. Ask my cousin booie or my cousin rude who went straight to the navy if we don't be getting all the ladies. Ready, set, go. Shake it like a ho. Jump on my thing and make it vibrated like the school ringing. Crawl underneath the sheets and get it wet like the eye of a little child crying. We get mo respect than all them fools who claim to be gang banging, dope deal slanging. Claim they got a pocket full of stone they better leave me the fuck alone they don't wanna get wrong they not even in my zone. And when I say who I ain't talking about Mike Jones. I'm taking about my cousin Julius. Who I said my cousin Ju. That guy can do anything that he put his mid too. Probably go straight to NBA and become the next Michael Jordan. Last but not less ask my Crandles how we do. Hit the club and flame up like one hundred candles. I ain't no piano. I ain't made to be play with like a lil child with toys. Better find you some toys or go get you some action figures before I release them triggers.

Nobody flyer than me.
() Nigga said he was flyer than me. I look at them screwy with a mean mug like Stewie. What the deuce. Do you really battle. Pull up to the studio and watch me get loose. Holy water step in the booty with more rhythms than Dr. Seuss. The realist in the booty and my faith is the proof make these wack rappers go poof. Lyrical, metaphorical, assembly, advanced rhyming ability. I should get a flow game scholarships. Pockets on swollen with Paul Bunyan money clip. Stack chips like casinos. Hip hop super hero. Flow sweater than sugar flavored cereal. Colder than sub zero. How you supposed to be a gangster rapper and never bust a pistol. Cause I don't stay on Earth I stay on Planet Imagination. In another galaxy like the galaxy trio. Spunk up and give these other rappers goose bumps like the ghostly trio. Plus I got a click full of and military disciples nickname teamo supremo. Open up my mouth and spit miracles like the red words in the bible. And niggas couldn't spit harder than me if got Young mike to slap the taste out yo mouth.

Tried of faking
() I tried of this fake until I make it. It's time me to step in game and take. Pimpin all the world Ludacris and Bobby Valentine. Hope in rage rover and brush the dust off my shoulders. A little rich boy with no limited but I ain't Lil Romeo. Half those dudes talking shit but they ass phony no good like spilt bologna. I'll never give up been through too fucking much. Touch sky. Just R. Kelly I believe I can fly. Get it popping like fireworks on the forth of July. Nigga I though I told you that we can't stop until we reach top. I'm ready to go global tell some body. It's not a secret like the amount money in somebody wallet. Take over the world and lock it up in my pocket like the pictures inside of a locket. Eat it up like its my bar of chocolate. Might not come when I want it but it will be here right on time. Even if I do not, did not become rapper or actor. I still will achieve great things. It's a lot of things in world both good and bad that either you or I desire to have happen. But we should always appreciated our blessing. Thank god for you got to get to what you want.

I'm one in a million
() I'm one in a million. Doing something you ain't seen. Smocking and smacking up on

that bumble gum weed. Say what. That's right. I be smocking and smacking up on that bumble gum weed. Plus that bumble weed got me going insane thinking I can move faster than a speed train quicker than a bullet just call me the matrix. more powerful than a locomotive. To be on top is my motive. Bounce like rubber. My shit going global its going to spread out like melted butter. Do it like none other. Dance like in you in club with holy ghost. This ship so good it make wanna slap yo mother. Powerful just like superman but I'm not allergic to kryptonite. I'm a ruff rider I'm going to party all night. Lil mama if you wanna you can take me home and ride me all night like a child on Christmas with a brand new bike. Guarantee to be so hi that flying like a kite. Blood fizzing through body like a shook up sprite.

Lyrical
() I got that lyrical, assembly, metaphorical, futuristic advance rhyming ability. You can call it technology. Shut down these rappers like a computer. Rap game ruler post on the throne like king copper. Know you think I'm playing with the big dogs but I'm King Koopa dinosaur. Hardcore gangster rapper but no my pants don't be sagging. Never catch me lacking. Never catch me sipping. Ball like London Tipton. Let me go browser through my note book and find a 16 bar killer. Not Michael Jackson but welcome 2 the thriller. Hotter than a fever. I suggest you bet it before my temper get heat you going to end up defend. Cock back squeeze the steal fire on the trigger. Make you hope around like Tigger. Plus I collect money like Winnie the Pooh collect honey. Haters on the side line looking at me funny. Slap that look off your face and make you change your expression. Isn't no bobby on level my whole swagger is a blessing.

The thought of losing you
() I can't bare the thought of losing her because she my one and only. Without her I feel so lonely. Like a baby without his mommy. Wonder if Adam felt this way in the gardening. Surrounded by all beautify with a look of confusion. Walking around looking all foolish. Wondering while he was feeling so useless. He had everything under his feet, even the beast were under his control. But he still was only half a men because he had half a soul. His life pass him by. Day by day and moment after moment. Because a men is not really a men until he finds a good women. Me and you go together like the DBZ fusion. My love for you is worldwide like pollution. Its love in the air somebody please tell me if you can smell it, can you taste it, can you touch it, can you grab it because I already knew that you want it. But is there anybody in the world who doesn't want real love unite. If your love was a ocean then I would be the harbor. If your love was a fast food restaurant then I would be the guy behind the counter saying "May I take your order." Me without you would cause chaos to whole order.

Different path
() Paper strength out like the neck of Jeffrey the toys R US giraffe. Collect mo green than a Christmas Elf. Flow so cold something like Jack Frost. Everybody want to be a thug but I wanna different like Robert Frost. Weather or not you call me nerd. Think I'm a Steve Urkel then I'm still going to diverged take a different path spit the game in half. Me and whoever else left. If you want to come join me then cross over to light side. The road less traveled. Softer surface, less gravel, and less traffic but with a lot more value. The status

of a queen or a king but you still going to be a server to the kings of kings the most high and mighty so if he be for than who can be against you. Therefore I'm the realest you ever seen. Just pull my resume and check my credentials.

Booty bounce like trampoline
() Booty bouncing like a fucking trampoline. Be so fresh and clean when I roll up the spot. Pockets full of green nick name me Listerine. Ya'll I already knew what I mean. Curves in her body shape like syrup bottle. Spin around like a beyblade hope in the escalade. Hottest girl in this place. Like the way her hips wiggle. She twirl and she whirl and hot just like a candle flame them other girls so lame. Show they ass how to do it. I promise you Cherish made that song when saw you do it, do it, do it. I need a girl with some these qualities. Patent, reliably and self independent. Know how to carry herself in public but when its quiet time behind close doors she don't hesitated to let me get up in it. Get inside yo body, mind, and soul. Take off yo clothes and I just lose control. You prettiest rose in the Garden of Eden. 24, 7. Morning, night and evening.

The future of hip hop
() Hey Yo! Its the future of hip hop. Frontiers of solitude. Garbrater. The new world order. Come around here and you will get your but straight slaughter. Riding down the boulevarde and I'm booming The Carter and our CD coming to be just as hard. Every song booming back to back even the interlude. Music circulating through the streets. You be vibing to the beat. Music circulate through your earlobes. If wanna battle get fold and scramble like a rubix cube. No! Not Ice Cube but today was a good day. I'm all about the Benjamins. Everybody wanna be a thug then go ahead and prove it. Compared to me you might be feminine. Because you ain't really got no evidence. My paper stacking like elephants be multiplying like germs. Plus when I see green I go . Chilling at Brandon house playing guitar hero. Me and Ryan playing guitar hero. Tomorrow I'm hang out with Justin and Jerry and I might call Kimberly. Now consider this a warning before I get sign and my album start dropping

Dumb it down
() I heard a song call dumb it down. Decide to turn it up. Make it erupted. Flow so sick it will give you the hiccups. Then make you throw up. I grew up and screwed up. Thinking that you badder then me is going to get you chop and screwed up. Screw and choop up. Don't get it corrupt I spited like I'm corrupted. Corrupted with evil talk in fire like Satan child the omen but men worst sin was always the women. Women worst sin is own self respect. View on reality. Individuality. Like trust me cuz. I seen the evidence like dudes who only look at the face and booty to see if you a cutie. What they know is that you might grow up and get upgraded like Rudy. But they won't experience that. Because they a dog that's scared of change you like Scooby. Run around in the streets playing with hoochies. All of em easy. Get em wet, bust em open and have them leaking like a broken jacuzzi . You ain't noting but a dog I tell you cause you drooling. You think you a player but really you just foolish. Because does it really count if all you fucking is hos.

Shine Like Sliver
() You shine like sliver and you glitter like gold. Sparkle like a star. Make music like a guitar. My heart beating in a rhythm. You look fine in whatever you wear work close or denims. I'm a student at Trenholm. O.K. that was totally off the subject, but its just so easy for me to talk to you. Drink water and start to dance probably make it rain. Put happy thoughts in my brain and joy in my heart. This joy in my heart the world didn't give it and the world can't take it away. Every time I come around you then its just a

better day. I'll play Jay-Z if you be my Beyonce. Got me dangerously in love but if loving you is wrong then I don't want to be right. These other don't fill up my appetite. They just appetizer while you main course meal. You the un-tray. Sex you so good that want an encore. Hit the mall and ball then buy out the whole store.

Haters

() Haters keeping on eyeing me. I don't know why they keep on trying me. Not gone to achieve anything but end up with anxiety. Glowing like a Christmas tree. Know that I got mo red beams than a Christmas tree. Do you really wanted to battle we can do like rice crispy treats. Snap crackle pop that glock to yo check. One round to the head will knock you off yo legs make yo ass go to bed. You dead wrong, dead wrong, now you dead and gone. Now you sleeping in a grave crib living in la la by by by. You so n'syne. U.g.l.y I'm aint excuse. Because my rhymes are so cruel. God dam adorious Fast and furious. Cruising in the fast lane looking for the fast cash moving like osmosis. Got my eyes on the prize and I keep picking up speed. You know I'm hell of focus.

I did and you did too

() I did and you did too. Everybody go through tears and suffering but a lot of other people had it worst than you do. People from New Orleans when hurricane Katrina hit Desire to walk around with facial expressions much meaner. Been back and forward to and from hell. But I plan on been bless cause I all ways do my best. Start walking with Jesus now I fell just like Kanye West and the day before I die I have to testify. Walk around with my head heal high come up in the spot looking extreme fly. I gotta testify. Wheater ya'll ready or not I'm about to touch the sky. But first I need a workout plan God lead me a helping hand. See someday I about to stand up own two feet and be a real man. Guardian angels on my side so I'm ready to ride. The sky is limit these other niggas frail and timid. If you pray while worry and if worry while pray. The sky was the limit but I couldn't see outside the box until I got more confidence and stop acting timid. No guts no glory the early bird gets the worm that's why I rise early. God is on my side so I'm walking out the door in a hurry. The world is yours for the taking. Watch me go and take it.

Magic Sheets

() By day I'm playing basketball at night I snatching off her draws, while she sucking up on my balls. Licking on yo body, caressing her body. Body feeling naughty sipping on pina coladas. Messaging on yo shoulders rubbing down your arm our love is sweater than lucky charms if its cold than we can cuddle up crawl under the sheets and get warm check out my magic charm. I got the magic stick my girl is the magic chick crawl underneath the sheets and watch us do some my tricks. Over here blushing showing my dimples act like as if I was shy. Its Dark as hell then I get to blushing and my face light up like Rudolph nose. Get me horny then my dick grow like Pinocchio nose. Popping off her bras and ripping off her panties. Turn off the lights and then take off yo clothes. Hit the mall and ball. If you want go get I'm buy it. Tell them other broke jokers be quiet.

I'm in my zone
() I'm in my zone so all you niggas leave me alone. Ya'll don't want to get wrong. This ain't baseball but the only you going to win is if you run you ass home. Capping bullets out gun watch them fly thought your dome. Watch as I do it big like nigga name Biggie. Stop tryina flask and show off. Fake as ice soft ass diamonds like pillows. Real diamonds suppose to cut glass that shit will barely chip grass. You think its funny not to have no money. I got carrots like Bugs Bunny. You pussy ass niggas be just as sweat as honey. So let me Winnie the Pooh. He a match for you. Shooting bullets in the room let them fly through air like zoom don't react too soon. Knock you sideways and let yo brains spread like dust being sweep with a broom.

Radical and ratchet.
() I'm radical and I'm ratchet. Power like a Super Saiyan. Glowing like Gohan. Nigga I'm the chosen one. Feeling like the golden child. Smocking like a black and mild on fire like a cigarette. But when it comes to music that say that I'm illiterate. Homie you talking inconsiderate. Home boy don't be ridiculous. I got back to back hits and I know you can't stand it. Boy I got that new, new. I'm heat like a barbecue. Keep on talking wrong then I will have you jumping like a kangaroo. I'm a beast up on the mic I eat it up like dog food. Nickname me Cujo. Mother fuck the gang rules. Represented the old school. How I'm going to afraid of a bunch of color coordinate ass niggas. Act like cheerleaders. Talk a lot of ship before it all go down but when its game time these niggas can't hang. That's really lame you onto to be shame. You must be gone insane thinking that you superman acting you steel. You softer as a banana and about to get peel.

Certificate
() Military minds certificate. Beneficiate. Rapping on the track with my nigga B-rise and my nigga D-dog. Fuck nigga realize. Screw with holy water and will get baptized. Stand up like you hard and you will fall just the like towers. Pussy little coward. Spray you like a shower. Linking for hours. Nigga I'm on fire like just like a candle. Spray you with that ammo. Shooting like Rambo. G.I Joe. Flow like Dro with a whole lot of hustle. Grand ass hustle. Hustle like Ross. Nigga I'm boss. Watch me stunned and watch me floss like a dentist. On fire like the phoenix. Menace like Dennis. Beat you back and forward like the little yellow ball when somebody playing tennis Venus and Serena. If I climb up my wallet up money then I will be somewhere up in Venus.

Jamacus Newton galaxy
() Its Jamarcus Newton latitude. Jamarcus Newton longitude. I feel like miss Patti Labelle I got a new attitude. And I'm on fire like hell. I spit magic like spells. You can gone call me Waverly. I'm smocking like a factory. Powered like a battery. Pimp juice flowing all through my anatomy. Jamacus Newton galaxy. Seven figure salary. Pockets on swole like clog up arteries. Military strategic strategies. X-factor skills agilities. Extraordinaire rhyming abilities.
Flow sweeter than cavities. I'm so fly I'm been hated on by gravity. That's why Sir Isaac Newton disclaim me. Cut me from the family tree like he don't' even know me. Well fuck it. You ain't gotta believe in me. I'm still going to sell out its guarantee like

warranty. Flow serious like warren G. Notorious like B.I.G. Plus I got a click full of military disciples go ahead and send it the cavalry. And every time I step to the mic it's a significant event like what had happen on Calvary.

Truth be told
() Truth be told. I was never a gangster that mean I'm a wangster. Bring new to the game I'm a stranger. I'm a rookie but I'm doing big boy numbers. Creep up on her and whisper in her ear and ask her for her number. Wait till you see my wow. Can't wait to put it yo hole. I'm about to lose control. Go ahead and take off yo clothes. Just take of yo clothes and so I can decorate yo body. Make yo body go num from yo head to yo toes. In love like Keisha Coles. Got me picking petals off a rose. She loves me so, yes she does. She loves now and she me loves later. That's my girl better bag back hater. Put my heart on fire make me blush got me shining like a lightsaber.

Guess what cuz
() Guess what cuz, you must not know who I be. I'm Lil JC with the class 2007. Graduated from JD. Half of these fools ain't ready for me. Be thinking I'm a little kid is gone to get yo did in. Every want to be thug but them dudes really fruity. Now bust a cap in they ass and put but 2 but cracks in they booty. Talk a lot do do, but when they saw me approaching got scared and scatter out roaches. All boosting and bragging. You ain't ready for no action. But when I come around they vanished like a ghost. Disappear like Danny Phantom and vanished funky phantom cause isn't no telling when that negro strike back and kill another at random. Pimpin take a look, please don't get it shock. I don't give a dam. I'm a straight out thug man. Snap yo girlfriend up like a professional crook. Watch you get flip like pages in a book. Take her home and take off her thong. Be an gentlemen or ride it like a roughrider you ugly as hell you need to hide yo face with a towel you stink and I smell like flowers. I made love to yo mom for an hour then hope in the shower. Came out smelling like flowers. Trying to whip my ass thinking that you bigger. Pull bullets out my trigger over here hustling trying to stack my figures. They talk a lot shit but I'm say its cause they blizzard. Specking like they blaze talking like they mouth was in a shit talking race. They just trying to showed off smack'em in the face and make they ass bruise. Face turn colors like a traffic light dude. Smack'em in the face start specking in a slow pact. Walk around with a daze look on they face. Better wake up and pay attention like the end of school days.

Posted up chilling
() Posted up chilling like the clothes on a hanger. You know that song made by Ciara. She a R&B singer. When it first come on this she started off singing "He he don't have his love sweet as honey." Well then I got bonus. I got money and my love is sweeter than cake. I will do whatever it takes to make your pussy wet like a lake. Rough sex make you feel like yo back about to brake. Get it shaking like a Earth Quake. I love you like a pimp love ho's. Ya'll ready know that my girl shine like silver, glitter gold, put Alaska on fire made hell caught a cold. Stone cold, ice froze. Make yo body quiver and shiver from yo head to your toes. Even though we got it heated like steam engine. You the number 1 girl on my team. Let me fulfill the desires of your dreams.

I believe
() I believe in making ever experience education. That's why through life with all the struggle. I stay learning, stay stunning, and stay turning. Hype like these the people off that chronic. Fly through this mug like sonic. I'm turn to knuckles if you still ready to rumble. You can get yo but crumble like a bag of Ruffs. You think you best but I'm still not impress. I'll hit you in yo back and make yo chest swell now you look like a nigga walking around with breast. All that stuff that you talking but I'll still not impress. They scary cause they not ready shacking like the fat on the Goonies. Let me see you do truffle shuffle. I think you kinda of Looney Tunie. You must not know who I'm is. I'm lil JC. Keep it banging like a drum line full of drummers. Vibrate like thunder. Fame up like a Bunsen burners. Release the fire. You don't won't battle I got the eye of the tiger I'm put you on trail. Now I be the jury so get ready for an execution that might be the solution to all this confusion. That confusion in you head, be thinking that you bad. I hate to break your spirit and crush it down like fractions but I'm lay you suckers out like the blanks on a matters.

Roses are Red

() Roses are red violets are blue. My diamonds is a bright color yellow. Same color as Bart. I'm blasting at them Mandarks. I'm a genius like Dexter caught me in my laboratory. I called it the studio and I'm cooking up glory. I got presidential status catch me chili in the house with my home boy Corey. On a mission to collect that green. Trying to dream up a scheme or plan or plot to make it the top. And as you can tell this is not Kenan or Kel. I won't stay in the middle because I would get caught because I ain't doing nothing illegal. I'm going to rise to the top. I'm off the meter and I'm off the charts. The cream of the crop and the future of hip hop. Lil Jamarcus Newton drop on it like a rain drop and make you do the bunny hop.

Just Remember

() Truth be told. I was never a gangster that mean I'm a wangster. Bring new to the game I'm a stranger. But just remember that thugs need love too. Of this I am sure. If you don't believe me just listen to Tupac Shakur. And since Pac pass away a lot of things these rappers say no longer matters today. And if your love disappear. Everything I do in life would no longer matter any more. That's we got to stay together. Always and forever. I just can't live without you. Stick to you like tattoo. Attach like paper and glue. I can't image what would happen if I lose you. You gave me chills like fatty koo. Absolute zero. Got shivers like I bath in snow. Made my heart grow like the Grinch. Every moment I spend with you is time well spent.

Superstar Jamarcus Newton.

() Superstar Jamarcus Newton. Open up my mouth and spit fire hotter than the devil's piss. I'm talk in flames like Luther. Plus I got money than Lex Luthor. Acting bad like Satan. I'm a beast, I'm a monster I'm a dog. With my teeth, my fangs, my claws and my paws. Plus my flow keep going even when the beat take a pause. Super rap now I feel Nas which means I'm a hero even if I ain't rocking nothing but some speedo. Kanye west ego. Flow something like Dro don't test me I'm a pro. Do you really wanna battle I think not. Come through like juggernaut make yo body go drop when you hear them shots go pop. Then you hit the ground like free throws. Crush like Doritos. Mo ice than a Eskimo and mo cheese than a Cheeto. You can't stop my flow and you can't stop my glow. Time to shift into turbo. Chili at Brandon house playing guitar hero. Mo flyer than magneto. Plus I got a crush on the chick from camp rock Demi Lovato.

Phone call

() Gun on the left side. Bandana on the right side. Bust you wide open and have u leaking like a slip and slide. Soaking like you baptist. Put a hole in yo mind and make u dizzy. Get silly. Now u looking surprise feeling like you hypnosis. What you don't realist fuck nigga I'm certified. I can tell you wanna cry. I can see it in your eyes. Where u think going hide. Where think you going run. Cause I will find you just like I found Waldo. Have my people come touch all u ho's. Get beat down like a drum roll. Got a line full of Goons that be longer than a railroad. Now yo whole body sore. And yo face looking soar and body parts swole. I got goons in every city, every hood, every ally. Shooting at yo belly blow a hole through yo belly button. Pop a few at yo feet and make you dance like teletubbie. So gone head punk and make my day if you feeling lucky. Mad cause you a rookie and you mad cause I'm a pro. And you can't stop my shine and you can't stop my glow. Time to shift into turbo. Put my eyes on the price and stare picking up speed. I'm that dude that got what you need. Shooting off yo knees and make you pray on yo elbows.

I don't mean to be rub
() I don't mean to be rub but I need for you to shut and listen. I love you like a black kid chicken. So please pay attention. Up there talking about we won't be together. Our love is forever. It can over come what ever. You can't deny it. You can't fight it. For the rest of life we is going to be united like X-men part 2. Stick to you like a tattoo. Forever I love you and that's guarantee the way its going to be. You and me go together like the branches on a tree. No other girl on Earth is want you worth. I'm going be your freaky lover. Time for me to stray up and make you bounce like rubber. Jump like Flubber. Catch the holy ghost and run around yo mother. Make you melt like hot butter. No one can do it better. For the rest of our life we is going to be together.

Not down with OPP
() I'm not the mail man but I bring good news. I got the killer data. Killer information naughty behavior. When I step to the mic. Like naughty by nature. You down with. O.P.P Naw! I'm too much of a gentlemen. If you don't touch my property then I won't touch yours. But if yours give it to me then it was her choice but not by force. I'm the king of the game and I don't have any remorse. Don't have significant. Sick ass receipt, love from my family and a whole bunch of friends with hell of flows. Killer bank rolls, clean ass clothes, classy ass ho's pockets on swole. Plenty of heat and the worlds best beats. Between the heat and the beats it don't what we use but you still going to move yo feet. Sit back and chilli and watch me eat up the beat. Specking of eating Lil wanyne is a beast feed him rappers or fed him beats. Plus I am a freak watch beat and make her leak. My name JC and I'm so unique my pocket on swole fatter than Monique. I got a cousin name Malik who has sister name Davida and before I end my verse I must say rest in peace to Aaliyah.

Shot first
() Shot first and talk later. Keep it moving like my CD in a CD player. One girl in and one girl out. They nickname me now and later. Why. Cause I'm in the mood now and I'm in the mood later. I'm get her now but I'm call your friend later. I'm going to stack my paper now and then stack my paper later. Ain't got time for no haters. And you can't play a player you going to end up getting play. Fresh to deaf in my green and gold. That's my JD school colors. I do it like no other. Cause I'm hot and you not and you really need to stop. Pockets stay with green and I'm heated like steam. Riding with a dime that look diamond, sun roof top and a gangster lean. And I stay with green plus I'm shining gold. Get it shacking a thunderstorm. Eating lucky charms. Stacking stacks taller than a min-men same size as a leprechaun. It's 32^0 degrees below freezing but I'm still sitting on warm because I'm just that hot.

I don't need nobody
() I don't need nobody else get me specking ying yang. I hustle all by myself. Nickname me the lone ranger feel I got powers like a power ranger. Why are you still talking to me? My mother told me not to talk to strangers. They got a lot of shit to say specking yak, yak. I don't really give a care. Everything they want to talk about is so, so, wacky. Smack'em in the head and punch'em in back. We throwing bows like Ludacris. This shit is so ridiculous. Why is they still talking to me. You don't know me like that. Got me specking like TI. Black his eye (ojoes nergos) and make them want to cry. My money so thick it strength out like my dick. So nigga try to name some shit that I can't buy. Who in the hell is this guy. Why does he think he fly but it's based on a lie. I said once before but I'm say it again. Get me feeling like Ludacris. Trick move! Get me yelling like TI. You don't know me like that! So move out of my way and bag back from my space before I hit you in the face and have you specking in slow pact.

Get real messy
() You don't wanna battle. You don't wanna do that. I will mess you up. Get real messy, tacky, raggedy. Like a doll name Ann. I ain't playing. But I will play you like toy. Steadily creeping. Ride up real slow face to face, face to face. Old fashion like the wild west. Then leave you with frustration when I blast you like cowboy moo mesa. Light you on fire like the sun. Shooting at you like my name was Trigun. Throw you away like a piece of bumble gum. Just ran out of flavor. Lit you fire now you blacker than Dark Vader. shining like a light saber. Collect mo green Yoda. Staying stack taller than a mini-man same size as a midget. I got mo bread than a biscuits. Put that orgasm in her belly and make her scream like she was yodeling.

Sit here and chill
() I'm going to sit here and chill. Cursing down the block with my head hanging by the window seal. Hype and shocking like an electric eel. Get dizzy like a over dozen of benadryl. Chilling like a villain act lazy like Garfield. Man my paper just stack up like hills. Then I get this pussy wet like a baby eating and drooling. I think you might need a bib. What's my adlibs. "Push'em to the floo and do the A-town stump right here smacked daple in the middle of the Gump." Hit the club and get crunk juice. Now it's tic-tac-toe. 3 in a row. Everybody get you ass up on the dance floor. Head, shoulders, knees, toes. Shoulders, chest, pants, shoes, stupid, fat, ugly, ho. Wipe me down, get gone, so long, see u later alligators. I ain't time for no haters. They not even on my level. Cause I'll blast with them pistils and kill yo ass 3 ways. Rock , paper, scissors. I make it rain. You make it sprinkles. Stay so fresh and clean like breath that just ate a bunch of altoids. Run and shot like cowboys . I ain't made to be play with like a lil child with toys. But I'll still play you like a toy and use you as my doll. Get real raggedy and tacky like doll name Ann. I ain't playing. I'll leave yo ass confuse like Alice in wonderland. Bend the top of yo body to the back of yo body and kill you like Pac man.

Booty real big
() Booty real big and her pussy feel like Jello. When we make love she can ride me like bike. Fly like a butterfly, sting like a bumble bee and float like kite. Blood fizzing through my veins like a shook up spirit. Turn off the lights and ride me all night like a child on Christmas with a brand new bike. Everything going go to be all right. I'm so, so hype. Ultra Hype Entertainment. Mason D Entertainment. We came out and we containing you fools in containment. Cause we the future of entertainment. Got me floating 9. Similar to Brandy because I'm sitting on top of the world. High as hell like I was on drugs, but since that I ain't the case then I must be love. All day long me and my girl is going to kiss and hug. Lay on her like bug on a rug. Girl you need a real a man so come be with me and stop fucking with these scrubs.

Equal opportunity employer
() I'm a equal opportunity employer so I'm also attracted to white girls. Let's have interracial love. You can called it jungle fever. And you can come play in my jungle like I'm Mowgli. I got a whale of a dick you can call it Moby. And you know its mighty Thor. Let make beautify music like Jimmy Henderson guitar. Or maybe Whitney Houston voice. And let me pet the kitty like Cee'Lo hand on the voice. Then fuck you all night like horse, And whenever it get moist I will have shouting like a choir in rehearsal. Fuck you all without any kind of rehearsal. Barely move a muscle. Flip it over from the back and then let you ride it. Call it role rehearsal.

Brand new to the scene
() Brand new to the scene but I'm so fresh and clean with a pocket full of green nickname me Listerine. Cuz I'm on top and you on the bottom. You not on my level I suggest you get a ladder. You came from the land down under but I ain't talking about Austria. You pussy eating mother fucker. Open up yo mouth and stick out yo tongue. I bet you still got a piece of kitten kit crumb left around yo gums. Come at you dropping bombs. I'm just like Lil Wayne in that destiny child song "You don't see me on the block I ain't tryina

hind I blend in with hood I'm camouflage." Its an mirage. I'm like the spider swinging from cobwebs in the back of that dusty ass garage. Nigga posted up chilling. Blend in with the background cause I ain't show off or flask. I got a bag of goodies but I'm not Santa Clause I hustle like Rick Ross. Nigga what's up. Man you can be boss. But you ain't even on level you more like the employee. I'm the golfer. You the caddy. I be stunna like my daddy but I was raise by my mother. Ain't that ironic.

Super trooper rough riders
() Super trooper rough riders. Float like hang gliders. Come through this mother fucker on fire like ghost rider. Wild out like Nick Cannon. Me and my nigga Brandon. Last name Murray. Floated like Kirby. Man you dudes wanna be thugs. Trying to make a check can fake it. I'm call my nigga David. So David grab the salt and point them in eye. Beat yo beat yo ass like Stewie and destroy your whole family guy. So freak fly. I'm James Bond super spy. You inch high private eye. Fly like a angel on fire like a demon. Me and niggia Jezzy stay with mo green than Luigi. On fire so we red like Mario dropping bombs like Wario. Ya'll people better know you get you ass bruise. Mo bruises than Dennis Rodman got tattoos. Don't make me act a fool. Me and my nigga old school also know as black pound. So best believe its going down. "Push'em to the floo and do the A-town stump right here smacked daple in the middle of the Gump."

Resist the temptation
() Truth be told. I was never a gangster that mean I'm a wangster. Bring new to the game I'm a stranger. Just remember that thugs need love too. Of this I am sure. Just listen to what Tupac got to saw. Today is my day. Didn't come here to play got me talking like R-jay. Don't need too many riches or a whole lot of wishes. As long as I get a girlfriend with plenty of chocolate kisses. Plus I think a pussy fetish cause my dick stay inching. Get it heat like chicken fresh out the kitchen throw it in the skillet. watch the grease bumble. Worlds best lover. Don't organism too soon. Start yo ass breathing like air escaping from a balloon. Swept you off your feet like broom. All this frustration trying to resist the temptation. I'm give you the world. You know you wanted to be my girl. If its cold outside then I got the month of May. Same month as my birthday. Gemini, stayed so fly. You the fines girl I ever saw with my eye.

Talking Gibberish
() Why you talking gibberish. Specking yak, yak and yo ass is really wiggity wack. I do not understand lame nigga talk. Don't understand what lame niggas do. So showed yo ass up deep niggia like an ant bed. Until I shot his ass in the head, lay his ass down dead. Stand still like a flat pillow laid on a bed. Please don't make me mad before I power up like a Super saying and get Goku on yo weak ass, ass. This shit so sad. Why must you act bad. If going whip my ass, whip my ass. What you waiting for. Gone head. Don't be scared let me see you break bread. If finna beat my ass. What you waiting for. Time is whining down. The clock going ticky-ticky-tock. You walk over here about to get yo ass straight mup-wump. Flame up like a candle. Hulk out and go Bruce Banner. Now "Push'em to the floo and do the A-town stump right here smacked daple in the middle of the Gump."

You not on my level
() You not on my level stop acting Ludacris. If you understand I'm walk up and talk to you just like Ludacris. Move bitch! Get out the way. Turn yo ass around make you suckers go the other way. Cause you don't want to battle. Get it shacking like a hyperactive retarded baby playing with a rattle. You might have a major malfunction. My paper connect together like conjunction. Now knowledge is power so let me educated you for a minute. The pen is mightier than the sword and I knew it because I didn't have to staple nobody. I put together pen and paper and wrote my ideas down then put them to beats. Now everybody moving they feat. Came a long way from banging on lunch room table 11 grade, 5th period Ms Siva class. Now let's fast forward time. Most cheerleaders got short shirt and no ass . Doing back flips on the grass. Kendra, Antoya and Jacinda 12th grade 5t period Ms. Canty class. If you understand I'm at the top of my class. The cream of the crop the future of hip hop. Drop on like a rain drop and make yo pussy pop.

Fine as wine
() Fine as wine, dam I want to get drunk. Your body's beating harder than those size 12's in my trunk. The sexiest girl, that I've ever seen. With a body like wow, she must be getting plenty of fibber. Your love keeps on taking me higher. So high that we might float in heaven. My ebony goddess, my Nubian Queen. Body so hot that I work up a sweat. I'd give my own life to make those panties wet. My love is the key, and your heart is the lock. Let me open up your soul, my pretty black fox. Drop on it like a rain drop and make yo pussy pop. When I hit your g-stop I promise I'll nerve stop. Beat it harder than a drum line, until pussy get num leave you in the bed having wet dreams thinking about me counting sheep sucking on your mother fucking thumb.

Put on a gimmick
() I'm not going to sit up here and put on a gimmick. Bold headed man wearing a toupée. All they doing is day dreaming. Day dreaming just like they Lupe. Plus I'm so cool. Mo cooler than Lupe. Plus I got leadership status nickname me commander cool. Catch me chilling coolsville with a pup named Scooby Doo. Freddy, Daphne, and Velma too. Yo girl, his girl, and yo bitch too. You wanna see how its done then you better watch them do them cause I don't really want you in my business. Amen, amen. Can I get witness. Come through and get it popping like chicken fresh out the kitchen. Throw it in skillet. Pop goes the grease. This is how I'm living just like thanksgiving. I'm thankful for living. Feeling like Krillin cause I got that destructo disk. Killer dope fly demo C.D. and a cool ass cousin who I hardly ever see and his name CD.

Now that I'm here
() Tried too hard to get here. Now that I'm here. I will not be move just like Rose Parks. Whoever said that my bark is worst than my bit was dead wrong. These people wouldn't be in my zone. You better put that shit in reserve. Never being scary like bone crush shooting bullets in the room. Let them fly through the air like zoom. Staring moving Usher but I don't think they ass is dancing. Over there talking about they a lover not a fighter. That shit really much matter. Pistols around my waist stuck to me like that paste. Do you really want to know how a mother fucking bullets taste. Just keep on talking shit get like that niggas in the club. Be like that nigga in the movie had to whip that trick.

Prove to the world that you is a bitch. Odds stack up against you but you have get on going. You have to think out box. Do the unpredicted like Jamie Fox. The situation going better. Somebody guarantee to hate on you but man forget about them. Ball you pinky and ball thump Hold three fingers in middle and tell them to read between the lines.

Chillin like a villain
() Chilling like a villain. Lay on the porch and act lazy. I know that you people think that ya'll is amazing. But if you bitches keep on talking nuts I'm go wild and crazy. Shot'em in the toe and having them walking with a limp like brand new pimp but niggia don't trip cause yo ass is just pip. That's P. I. P or you just be an imp. That's an I. M. P Cause you can never be like me. SO if they must, then they must. Keep on talking all shit until they fucking lips turn into rust then I must pull bullets out my gun and be ready to bust turn'em into dust. Politely pick up the phone and call his mom so she can come vacuum his ass up. So nigga what's up, why you acting stuck up, be ready to man up, you ran out of luck. You know that I'm so smooth and nice. Dudes like to call me cup the way I stay with ice.

David beat Goliath
() So what if I'm a lil nigga. Big niggas get laid down to. David beat Goliath with slingshots and boomerangs. I'm going to knock yo ass down with gun shots and bullet wounds. Put a hole in yo stomach and make his ass vomit. Now shoe off they belly don't look like a jelly fill with holes. Let these niggia know that I'm the star of the show. I'm king of the jungle just call me Simba. They ain't even on level. They ain't smooth criminals not like me and Michael Jackson pockets full of emeralds. Make these niggas shake and tremble. Cut yo ass do like a tree and yell out timber. I'm best at what I do. I suggest you remember. So you never forget me. Naw. You not finna forget me. I'm too important. I'm the king of the hill, the price of valley. The kingpin of rock. The god father of pop. The Frank Lucas of gospel. The James bond of country. The Don Wand of bebot. The cream of the crop. The sacrifice of R&B and the ring leader of hip hop. Plus the over all future of entertainment in general. Period.

Stand on block
() Stand on block and hit curve. When the car swear to the neighborhood where your ass belong. As soon as you ride up to my home that's when them pistols blast and you be lay on some red grass. You be lent up like Christmas tree. Then them witch up and fly away like a goose just as soon as the artilleries let lose. Stop thinking you bad. Before I'll chocked you with them dreads and leave you dead. Tied you on top of a light post with yo feet hanging, dangling 12 inches from the floor. I don't mean to brag but this shit is sad put bullets in your bladder. You ain't on my level gone to fuck need a ladder. Get fold up like a rag and put in a body. If they must, then they must talk all shit until fucking lips turn into rust then I must pull bullets out my guns turn them niggas into dust. Politely pick up phone call Whitey and Bobby so they can come sniff you ass up.

Phenomenal Men
() It's a new phenomenon. New pneumonia. I spit that sick flow. That disease. It might

make you ears throw up then I'm strap up. Put a saddle on yo girlfriend back then tell her to getting up. Plus when I see green go. I spit that ill flow. Its so cold or I could turn it into lava. When I spit the fire. I make it strike like lighting. You seen that carton the avatar. I'm floating like bishop if you want to go war then you can get attack like Viking now finna to go war. U got in too far now you stuck like tar. And can't you move. guarantee to lose cause trick I'm gonna win.

You got a lot to say
() You got a lot to say. You talk a lot of stuff. I think you mouth need sanitary. I'm well supply like the military. I suggest you find sanctuary. You got a lot to say. You talk a lot of do, do. Nickname you mouth toilet and no matter how many times I flush that stuff just won't go down. Nickname me fingers plumber ball me up ad make a fist. And then I hit like this. Have you specking like Lupe Fiasco now you talk like this. I knew this dude name Eddy that rock blue diamonds the same color as Eskimo piss. But check out the ice on my risk. Watch how it glisten. Got my finger tips froze. If I poke up in the nose it will make yo ass catch a cold.

Woke up this morning
() Woke up this morning. I was feeling kind horny. Booty Call! Call Lil mama over and I'm ripping off her panties and popping off her bra. From the window to wall. Till the sweat fall down yo vague she got that chocolate pussy it be feel nice and gushy. Got me playing with her tushy. Bend over shack that ass. Stick it in yo ass and make you feel it yo back and put it in your vertebrate. Feel it in yo brain and stimulate your intellect. Increase yo intelligence tell me can you handle that. Tell me if u like it like that. Lay you flat on yo back and make yo kitten cat go spit splat. Fucking you like a male ho but giving you much respect. As much respect as a real women suppose to have. For real though.

Just listen to what I say

() Just listen what I say. Hey DJ put my recorder on and keep it spinning like my rims. Hating on me but fuck them do the impossible like Kim. Get yo ass slice and dice and cut like a haircut trim. Hate on me but I won't stop not until I make it to the top. Getting it banging like a nail being hammer shine brighter than the flash on a camera. Pippin be smart I kept this mother fucking rolling like the prices at wal-mart. But I don't never go back I always forward. Float like a butter fly and sting like a bee. Fuck with me and I'm hit yo ass harder than Bruce Lee. Notorious like Biggie hit the club like Will Smith now every body getting jiggy. Ain't really gotta be to picky hit the club and find a chick and then take her home. Let her grind on me while we listen to pretty Rickey, Rickey, Rickey. I bet you I wake up with a hickey, hickey, on dickey.

I know you supposed to be a thug

() I know you supposed to be a thug. That's why you posted on the side of the corner with your lil mean mug. But it really don't mean much. Cause you still going to lose and I'm going to win. I'm post on the other side of the corner with a smile and a grin. So why you looking so mean and I stay grinning like Joel Osteen. Is it because I shine and I stay with green. That why they call me the Green Lantern. I beat like I was in the justice league and let yo blood spread out yo body flees. So what the business gone be. I'm go street fighters on ass and kick you Chun Li. Brand new to the game but I'm classified as a classic. Take something that's all there and flip and call brand new. Just like Stan Lee and Tyler Perry do. And those my idols. Watch me go wild like idle. Open up my mouth and spit miracles like the red words in the Bible.

Get jiggy with it
() Notorious like biggie. Hit the club like Will Smith now every body getting jiggy. Ain't really got to be to picky hit the club and find a chick and take her home and let her grind on me while we listen to pretty Rickey. Leave the club with 3 or 4 hickey. Hope in the escalade and ride all day. Take her to my place and now she ready to get laid. Cause I cut like blade slicing vampire. I'm going to knock it out the park like the umpire. Beat it and get heated like fire. To be on top is my desire. I'm the man of the hour. My shit going global like electricity moving through a telephone wire. Flame up like a lightered. Now I'm really, really tried of staying broken. They taking me as a joke. I'm trying to make my paper stick out like the belly of Al Roker. Sit back and chili while I'm smiling like the Joker. Messed they ass up like little child coloring. Go outside the lines. Get ugly like that song that Bubble Sparks wrote. Stunning like baby that's the number one stunner. Tunna in a minute I'm the number one tunna. Beat on yo head like professional drummer. Get you like that movie make you dump like dumb and dumber.

You don't want to battle
() You don't want to battle cause I get it shacking like a hyperactive retarded baby playing with rattle. And it's not hard it's simple. Poking dimples in yo dimples and holds in through yo grills. You really ain't that trill. Not for real. Then show me what the business is. Hit you in yo jaw and have you specking like Boomhauer from King of the Hill. Cause you all ready know who it is. You ain't on my level. Stop participating in false actives. You dam well you don't have the utilities or futilities to come close, to comparing to me.
Cause you the type the person who wanna be gangster to empress everybody. Be in back of club scooping out the scene looking for a nigga that feel should be lame nigga. Then you walk over be hoping and praying that they gonna jump back and acted scary trying to fly away like a mother fucking fairy. But them be the same niggas put bullets in you like the seeds on a strawberry. Now you feel like Jim Carve in movie get dumb and dumber. Making stupid decisions. Be tryina judge a book by its cover is going to get you in problem. Then you be oh ouch. Why you shot for. Because you'd a bitch ass ho. And I can't believe you asking me these questions. Smack them in the back of the head and yell out stupid slap.

Real nigga roll call
() Real nigga roll call. Shout out to Lil Dro. He the best thing smocking. I'm best nigga stroking. Girl I got that potion take a sip of this and put your back in motion. Bady we stroking it with the motion. I'll smooth like lotion. Our love is sweater than frosty flakes. I like that way yo ass shack. Thick as thigh, turn on some Uncle Luke and get ready a dickey ride. Turn around and make my eyes open up wide. Sexually attraction got me

about to break the matters. Make your pussy wet until the bed start leaking sweat. Sexually attraction guarantee to leave you with 99.9% satisfaction. 13 organisms, fuck in 12 different position in 9 different direction. Maybe two to three times a day. I know you like that way.

Watch as I glow
() I' m a pro watch as I glow. Don't never move slow. Cause I got a need for speed but I ain't talking about the game. No shame in my game. Be so fucking off the chain. Nick name me Holy Water so when it rain I bring the pain. Cause that's my element trying be on my level but that shit you doing ain't relevant. Hold up my nigga. All that breathing and blowing. All that huffing and puffing. All stressing and cussing. You ain't the bad big wolf is. Get me heated like a Jacuzzi. You ain't no bad jazz like Lil Boosie. Every body can't go zoom, zoom. Nigga don't react too soon, soon. Before I cause a typhoon, typhoon and got his ass breathing like air escaping from a balloon, balloon. Make it flood have yo ass dripping out blood. Get respect where ever I go but I don't have to gangbang or thug. Every body showing me love. I don't make to many rivals hold my peace next to my Bible. Said that I was Wangster while they claim to be Gangster. Went and compare themselves to 50 cent. So I flip these fools over like 2 quarters cause that's all they worth. Rise up like the sun and step on my turf. Get yo ass smack down to size like a little bit Smurf and fuck up they growth. You think 50 that nigga from G-unit. Then gone head, don't be scared, bring your gangster crew. But if I shot 9 times you won't live enough to see bullet #2. Trying to against me but O, I think like me. Let's put they ass in check like they was fucking made by nick.

Speaking alien
()You won't believe what I'll doing. When I tell you going to freak out. Because I'll smocking and smacking up on that bubble gum weed. I'll riding down the hood getting pull over by the police. They talking about they see smock and smell weed. I open up my mouth and all I got is gum, I be chewing on gum like is um, um yum. Chewing gum is my new habit. Man I just can't help like a brand new crack addict. Man I'll trying to work at it. Chewing gum is my new habit I just can't help like a brand new rack addict but I'll trying to work at it. I been chewing on this gum so long that mouth went num and tongue turned around got me speaking like Paul Wall be sitting. I be talking sit ways. Now everybody call me ET cause everything that I speak sound like I'm commuting with aliens. I'm too handle, I'm on fire like a candy, light up like Christmas tree. Man understand what I'm saying I ain't time for no playing. Talking shit like yak, yak and yo ass is so wacky, wacky. So when ever you ready to rumble. When ever you quit acting humble. Better not come with all that drama before I pick up yo mama and bet you over the head with her. Before I pick up yo mama and bet you over the head her.

Quality women
() The Q-is for quality, The U-is us, The A-is adventure, the L-is love, the I-is for intelligence, the T-is for trust and the Y-is for you, who I love some much. They come in different sizes shapes and varieties. But I need one with some qualities. I need the kinda girl that I can show all my love. They say it's some one out there for every body. So as I look out the window, my mind starts to wonder as the clouds filled thunder where hell could she be. My one true love. When I find her what the hell is I'm going to say. Imagine what she look like she probably got long curvedly hair sweet Carmen brown skin pretty ass toes that showed when she wore flip-flops. Little bitty tank top shirt on her parents couch lip locking. Hurry up and go to work let me bet it till it hurt. Rip the panties. Take off the shirt. Got me sprang like T-pain watch me rain like Lil Wayne. Liquid fluid coming out of yo vague. Sexy ass girl I can't wait to find her. Take her home Unzip her pants and take her out like dinner. It's that trill bust a nut in you liver let it flow through your river. Make it wet like typhoon. Organism too soon and start yo ass breathing like air escaping from a balloon. Hit the living room and do the bed room boom. It don't even matter we can do what ever you want. Because I'm here to please and satisfy yo needs. Be cool like a winter breeze. Make yo legs spread like the germs on a sneeze. Achoo!
Bless you! Baby please. What's wrong. Ain't no need to pick the telephone and call on Tyrone. Cause I'm right here when you need me. Just Michael Jackson use to say "just look over your shoulder baby and I'll be there." Lila mama fuck beaver just leave it up to me.

Bubble gum weed
() I'm one in a million. The crunkest dude in this place. How come. Cause I'm doing stuff you ain't never done. What it is. I'm smocking and smacking up on that bubble gum weed. Say what? That's right! Plus that bubble gum weed got me doing all type of amazing shit. Niggia want to cool so they come around here acting a fool. Wanna clown I'm clown with yo ass. Lay'em on some red grass. Sit yo ass over there in chair I don't give a care. Opposite of them dam bears with a tattoo of a heart on they chest. You keeping on talking all that shit until yo ass get breathless. It's going really dangerous and reckless. While you trying shine with wal- mart glitter cheap ass necklace. Use to call me Peter Parker the way I swing around the city with my friend Mary Janie be so fucking off the chain. Bubblegum weed got me going insane. I can't be Lil Wayne cause I never make it rain but can make her drop it like its hot. Fall down on it like a rain and make you do the bunny hop.

Love letter
() Write you an old school ass love letter in a gangster way. It be roses are red and violet are blue are blue. Make you feel brand new. Stick to you like tattoo. I like hugs and kisses. What about you. You so sweet and I love you too. roses are red and violet are blue thugs need love too. I like you. You like me. Let's get together and make baby. With some dick and some sperm and some egg and some pussy. Oh my God! I can see the head. Cause I like you and you like me. Let's get together and have a family cause the way I love you is the way you need to be love. Won't you say you love me too.

You and Me wedding Poem

(v1) Sometimes I sit at home alone with my head bobbing but even Batman had Robin. Although I'm use to being solo and I had a bless life it's now time for me to become even more blessed when I settled down and find me a wife. I'm have a little problem. I need some help on the double. I'm having a problem finding the one that should be my lover. They say it's some one out there for every body. So as I look out my window my mind starts to wonder as the sky fills with thunder where is my true love. With skin so soft like feathers from a dove. Looking like a angel sent from heaven above. There she is my one true love! I think this time she is the one that I going to marry. Wait a minute, I'm not ready for marriage. Just the thought of it makes me feel all scary. Wait a minute man! Get over your nerves this might be my only chance to find my one true love!

(v2) I must be in love cause I see shapes in the clouds. I feel so proud. Everybody else talking loud. I'm looking into your eyes but I'm staring into your soul. Feel like time slowed down. I ain't worried about the crowd got me smiling like a clown. Heart beating like drum, make my whole body go num. I want to stroke my hands all through your hair. I want to you kiss while our love is in the air. Without you it seems just so unfair. It not hard it's simple. I like to make you laugh and giggle like a little child being tickle just so you can show off your dimples. Massaging on your shoulders, rubbing down your arm, our love is sweeter than Lucky Charms. If it's cold then we can cuddle up. Crawl underneath the sheets and get warm. I get to blushing and my face light up like Rudolph's nose. I must be in love cause when I'm with you every thing feels so nice. You make my body shiver like I bathe in ice. Blood flowing through my veins like a speeding train. You and me go together like the wind and rain.

By: Jamarcus C. Newton
Date: 5/17/06

What's greater than together?

I guess you would have to be me to understand, how I knew this girl for two weeks, but already fallen for her like Steve did Laura. It's something different about her. It's like she got a whole new kinda of beauty. She got world going backwards, head spinning in circles, and heart banging like thunder. All I do is sit here to ponder and wonder. How could a guy like me find a girl this wonderful? Her kisses taste like strawberries, body so extraordinaire, and spirit extraordinary. The fact that she likes me it must be a miracle. And when I'm not around her I feel all frustrated and irritable. Knowing she could have any body she wants got me feeling kind of inferior. That's why I do best to succeed in supplying your wants and needs. That's why I don't have a problem rolling up my sleeves and dropping to my knees because I already know that keeping you satisfied won't be an easy. But I think that you worth it so I putting in the effort. Plus anything that you happy also make me feel better. And every time I come around her, she just get all slimily and gladder. I m not saying that it's meant to last forever but for the moment I can't think of what's greater than together?

Dedicated to: My true love
Written by: Jamarcus Newton
Written on: May 30-June 23, 2009

Saturday
Time: 9:51
June 3

My first love happy birthday

I'm wishing you a bless life and a happy birthday. It's your birthday so its on like white on rice, a glass of milk, and a paper plate stuck in a snow storm while a person rubbing lotion on they ashy arms. When I saw who I ain't talking about Mike Jones. I'm talking about Winnie the Pooh. The friendly little cuddy bear that can do any thing he puts his mind too. A lot people say he gay. He just likes to run around and play. If anybody gay is that little boy Christopher was his name, so lame. No dude should ever wear shorts that shorts that short. Them some daisy dukes. He cross leg when ever he eat fruit loops. Sit down at table like a lady. Ms will you be my baby. I love you like Winnie the pooh love honey. I ain't rich with a lot money. Just give me a chance to advance my stance. I'll give you everything you need. If you was with me I'll treat you queen and everyday gone feel like you birthday. Take you on a magic carpet cruise. I'm going to do you like Aladdin did Jasmine. Hope on that midnight train like Gladys. Party hats and banners. Get it jumping get it bumping banging like a nail being hammer, shine brighter than the flash of camera when somebody take a picture. Stop being modest it's the (Fourth) 4th of August. Show off and flask more than Santa Clause. Let these suckers know that you boss. Get this bumping and make them jump like Kriss Kross. Do it your way like usher do it my way on yo birthday. Let it burn and flame up like the candles on a birthday cake. It's 7:00 O' clock on the dot let's get the party started. Let's get rocking. Who is that knocking. Everybody wants to come in and join the party. Sipping on Pina coladas while handing out birthday dollar. Do it like that. Because you can do whatever you want to. Act a fool if you want. Show them how to do it. Cherish made that song when she saw you do it, do it, do it. When the theme music start to play just listen to what I say and do the booty bounce just you was Beyonce. *My first love Happy Birthday* I hope you like your gift. Might not have been much, but I hope it makes your spirit lift. I'm wishing a bless life and a happy birthday. God bless.

Dedicated to: My high school crush

JC Poems

My Forever Valentine

(v1) I saw you on the other side of the room and all I want to do is walk over and sweep you off your feet like a broom. But what if I walk over acting like I'm cool but you think I'm a fool and I get my ego bruise What if you say no and make me want to cry. Filled my heart with so much pain. Only you can stop my tears from falling rain. I can't even visualize why in world you would want say no. I'm the perfect guy for you to date. I will do whatever it takes. Do you like Aladdin did Jasmine and take you on a magic carpet curse. Treat you like a queen and show you a whole new world. Girl I'm telling you the truth. I'm sending you this love letter as proof.

(v2) I want you to be valentine. I can't even lie. I can't deny. I'm trying to get at you like a star in the sky. I not reach it but I can't help but try. I never meet a girl like you. You got over blushing showing off my dimples acting as if I was shy. I wish this was kindergarten, cause things were always so simple way then, way back when. When all I had to do was write a check yes, check no box. Now I am in high school and that would be un-cool make me fell like a fool. I can't do it any more. All the hell with it. I'm going to do it any way. Just keep on the down low. Don't anybody else know. Cause time is moving fast sand dripping through my hourglass. I don't see no other way. Nevertheless, it's about time to quiet all this talking and jump started to point. Would you like to be my valentine check yes or check no and let a brother know.

I Got the Victory

( ) I'm not Yolanda Adams and I didn't play in the gospel, but I got the victory stay up tall like a tree. I'm victorious, I'm glorious. I'm not biggie but I'm also notorious so watch as I do it big and go down in history. State my opinion like Martin Luther King cause both of us had a dream in the middle of the night while I sleep, while I dream, trying to make up a scheme. Come through with my crew, my click, and my backup, family and so call friends. Nevertheless, when nobody else is left then I am going walked by myself. Singing the tone to my favorite Psalm. As I walk through the valley of the shadow of death. I will fear no evil for thou art with me. Wow, hold up that's a enough! You all already know where I'm going with this. So really, men do not act surprise looking at me all mean eyes like Maya Angelo still I raise. They stay mad cause I not rich but I flask like a drug dealing man. I will nerve sell dope all you need is Jesus and a little bit of hope. I once hear a preacher say that the faith of a mustard seed will make mountains move out the way. I came here today to say to put Jesus first. The word of God is free to everybody and should not be kept a secret like what is inside a woman's purse. Causes see you can do anything through Christ that strength you. That's why I got the victory today.

Se Someday

() Sometimes life just seems so unfair. Like no body else but you cares and you fell like ripping off all your hair. You say to yourself what deal my life cannot be really. Well don't despair. Cause I have good news. Gods loves you so much that he sent his only son for who ever believes in him will not perish but have ever lasting life. So whenever a hater looks at you all mean eyes just remember what I said and began quote John 3:16. Because Jesus on my side and I will never give up hope and yes some day there will come a day that he will spread the bad from the good and se someday I will not have to live in hood. Se someday I will over come this divorce and take my life back from the devil even if I have to use force. Se someday I will over come this illness and then stop drug dealing. Se someday I will over come Sickle Cell and walk around with my head heal high and a story to tell. Se someday I will out due Cancer catch the Holy Ghost and start moving like a profession dancer. Se someday I will overcome this addiction and get up off behind stop reminisce be wondering where did my life go wrong because it's still not over until I'm dead and buried in stone I don't have to live my life so wrong. Se someday I'm going to take advantage of this gift God gave us call the ability to talk. So I'm going to stop being a liar and do something positive like sing in the church choir. Se someday I'm going to stop coming to church and pretending like I'm paying attention when I'm really not and start being in church events not just the benediction. Se someday I not going to walk out of church raising heck on a Monday through Saturday come back acting all holy on Sunday pretending like I got victory standing up tall like tree and God can straight through me. Se someday I follow rules and finish school and walk out a success thank God that I am bless. I will nerve fall down like Humpty Dumpy and if did I mighty become all lump, but that's still O.K. for a saint is just a sinner who ran out luck feel down and got right back up. Started my life off ugly just like that little duck then turned to swan at end start a brand new trend. Put Good and you guaranteed to win. Se someday everything will go my way.

Panther Power

() God bless the world with this dude name Malcolm. He had the X factor. Through his leadership rose up a group of black who represent the struggle. They tried to do something positive with their life but because the system was all corrupted, they establish a plan of sabotage and later on in life they quietly faded away just like a mirage, but I have good news because they are tough like stones they couldn't be silence for long. Scatter all over the world in undercover just like pollution but they are not trying to destroy it. They are trying to help save it. Be part of the solution and not part of the problem welcome to the revolution. Shout out to Panther Power!

Planet Imagination (JCN's Video, Music, and Story publishing)

Title of ownership/Company overview

Planet Imagination is an entertainment production and publishing company that was created by its CEO and founder Jamarcus Cordel Newton. To date Jamarcus is a student attending Alabama State University majoring in communication. He is 23 years of age. He currently lives in Montgomery Alabama. The company is personally funded and operated by Jamarcus.

The company specializes in the following attributes:

Film editing

Directing

Writing(short stories)

Book and magazines publication

Web Page design

Video and Music production

Animation

Drawing

Voice over work

(Writing)Song lyrics

Etc.

Rights of Content:

This document gives Jamarcus Newton ownership of Planet Imagination. It outlines the basic details of the company. All works including: short stories, song lyrics, videos, songs, etc are of original content. All products associated with Planet Imagination will contain any official Planet Imagination tag or symbol. The company holds the right to publicly distribute any of its products at any time. If the company uses all ready own or previously copy written material to produce a product, it will not override the previous owner copyright; however, it will allow protection of the work being produce; therefore, releasing it self of any copyright infringement. For example if a music artist uses a beat already own by a individual or label to record a record a song for their mix tape the original producers own the beat but artist owns the song that he or she has recorded.

If the company uses already own material to produce a new product it may still distribute its products as long it is not profit driven. If a product is distribute for profit permission of the original owner will be needed before distribution. Since the actions of the clients can be monitored on a 24 hours basics the individual client or clients who own product will be held responsibility for their actions not the company.

Stage Names:

Anyone who works with Planet Imagination is allowed to have any stage name desired. A stage name, also known as a screen name or showbiz name is a pseudonym used by performers and entertainers such as actors, wrestlers, comedians, and musicians, etc. A person may have as many stage names as they wish. It is up the individual to make sure that the stage name they have chosen is not already taken; however, the individual is allowed to have the same stage name as another person as long they can distinguish themselves apart and do not promote themselves as the same person.

The name "*J-Water*" is the official name stage name of Jamarcus Cordel Newton.

Tags and symbols:

All products associated with Planet Imagination will contain any official Planet Imagination tag or symbol. Tags and symbols are keywords, phrases, objects, pictures, or any particular mark that represent something by association, resemblance, or convention. Tags can consist of the words Planet Imagination showing up in videos or a voice recording of the words Planet Imagination being included in songs. Bearing or marked a specific product with the proper label usage is a way of giving ownership to a product or service.

The following image has been classified as an official Planet Imagination Symbol.

Right of Clients:

Clients are consider any one who uses a Planet Imagination product or service. If your face, name, voice, writing, or drawing appears on a Planet Imagination product you are automatically consider a client. Since Planet Imagination has the right to distribute all its products public at any time being a client gives this company the right to distribute a product containing any client identify. If a client does not wish to be seen as a public figure they must specify it with the owner before the product is produce. The company will not purposely damage anyone's character.

Payment:

Since the company is personally own and funded it does not have funds needed for normal scale employment at this time. Employees are hire on need only basic. Payments will vary depending on funds and the type of work the employee does, how much work the employee does, and quality of their work. Every employee will have their own personal contract discussing their payments.

Planet Imagination is operated from a home base location therefore it has a very selective cliental. Only those displaying a descent quality of character are select. Cliental is personally pick by the owner. Because its personally location and cliental the normal charge fees for using a Planet Imagination product or service vary and on many occasion clients are allow use service free of charge. For those clients who will pay a contract of agreement will be drawn stating the amount paid for the work done. Charge fees will vary depending the type of work being produce, length of work being produce, and time taken to produce the work. The company maintains right to charge whatever price is needed to maintain satisfactory profit.

Once the company relocates to a new permanent address where business can be done just as smooth and with a more peace of mind it will establishment standard rates and specific charge fees will be set base on the kind of service(s) needed, these new rates are still subject to change as need for profit however all changes will still be standard meaning all clients will pay the same prize for the service(s). Under certain and special conditions clients may also receive payment. Normally clients do not receive payment, payment will only be made if the owner Jamarcus Newton or a current employment requests outside assistance of that client to product a personal product of interest. There will a personal agreement contract draw up between that client and the requester. If the requester and client cannot come an agreement that project will be cancel. If a client wishes to receive payment for their contributes they must let the owner know before the production of a product; however, the company will have the right to not only denial payment, but the use of service as well.

Planet Imagination
(JCN's Video, Music, and Story Publishing)

Rights of permission

The following people have granted Jamarcus Newton doing business as Planet Imagination permission to use my vocals or lyrical material on the following mix tapes or album tracks. We have heard and approve of the tracks in questions. Zero ($0.00) payment is expected for my contributions for the projects listed below:

I __Michael Gripson__ (print name),
stage name: __Michael Dyer__

I __David Quinn__ (print name),
stage name: __David Qu Bones__

I __Bryan Dennard__ (print name),
stage name: __B-low__

I __Kaleb Dean Williams__ (print name),
stage name: __Meek Kais Dean__

I __JERRY OGBONNAH__ (print name),
stage name: __Jerry Ogbonnah__

I_____(print name),
stage name:_____

I_____(print name),
stage name:_____

I_____(print name),
stage name:_____

I_____(print name),
stage name:_____

I_____(print name),
stage name:_____

I_____(print name),
stage name:_____

Projects

Projects

Mix tapes
New Fly Spit The Mix tape
My Biggest Fan Is My Mirror The Mix tape
My Own Dimension The Mix tape
Will Rap 4Food The Mix tape

Mix tape material may be found on the following sites by typing the title in the search bar: Mixconnet, datpiff, mixtapepass, etc.

CD's for Profit
New Fly Spit
My Biggest Fan is my Mirror
Heartbreak Journey

Profit CD's may be purchase through the following sites by typing the title in the search bar: Amazon, Itunes, Cdbaby, Reverbnation, etc.

Right of permission for art work

I_____(print name) Stage Name: _____ certify that I have granted Jamarcus Newton doing business as Planet Imagination permission to use the following pictures. The pictures in question have already been exchange between the company during a private business exchange the artist and the company owner, no other pictures than the ones chosen that day may be use. At this time payment has been made nor has a price been set as to the payment amount. Payment is expected to be made in the near future for the use of the pictures. (Not yet sign, To be sign by Brandon Murray)

Brandon Murray Biography

Brandon was born on December 31st 1988. Attended Floyd middle magnet school for arts. In the 10th grade he transferred from BTW magnet high school to Jefferson davis. He won multiple art related awards and was later accepted into Troy university. He is currently the schools head cartoonist for the weekly paper.

Company Promise

If any other person appears on a track being use by Planet Imagination whether for profit or not planet imagination will take all responsibly for their likeness. Any person appearing on any of the above projects whom has not given the company permission to use their vocals or lyrical material as evidence show by this document may be consummated if they so wish. The company promises to no longer use another person vocals or likeness without their permission before completion of an product if it does so it may be held accountable for all actions.

Last updated: January 15, 2011

Certificate of Registration

This Certificate issued under the seal of the Copyright Office in accordance with title 17, *United States Code*, attests that registration has been made for the work identified below. The information on this certificate has been made a part of the Copyright Office records.

Maria A. Pallante

Acting Register of Copyrights, United States of America

Registration Number

PAu 3-550-146

Effective date of registration:

May 5, 2011

Title

Title of Work: Planet Imagination

(JCN's Video, Music, and Story publishing)

Completion/Publication

Year of Completion: 2011

Author

- **Author:** Jamarcus Cordel Newton, dba Jamarcus
- **Pseudonym:** J-Water
- **Author Created:** music, lyrics, musical arrangement, text, editing
- **Work made for hire:** No
- **Citizen of:** United States   **Domiciled in:** United States
- **Year Born:** 1988
- **Pseudonymous:** Yes

Copyright claimant

Copyright Claimant: Jamarcus Cordel Newton, dba Jamarcus
1242 Seth Johnson Dr., Montgomery, AL, 36116, United States

Rights and Permissions

- **Name:** Jamarcus Cordel Newton
- **Email:** jamarcus.newton@gmail.com   **Telephone:** 334-306-6787

Certification

- **Name:** Jamarcus Newton
- **Date:** May 5, 2011

STATE OF ALABAMA

MONTGOMERY COUNTY

CONTROL NO. 0312030120

LICENSE NO. 0003945

ACCOUNT NO. 030120

ISSUED TO:
PLANET IMAGINATION JCNS VIDEO MUSIC & STORY PUBLISHING
1242 SETH JOHNSON DRIVE
MONTGOMERY, AL 36116

LICENSE YEAR: 2011-2012

DATE ISSUED: 11 / 08 / 2011 (MO. / DAY / YR.)

LICENSE TYPE	
STORE LICENSE	
CHAIN STORE LICENSE	
OCCUPATIONAL LICENSE	X

BUSINESS LOCATION:
1242 SETH JOHNSON DRIVE
MONTGOMERY, AL 36116

EXPIRES September 30, 2012
RENEW IN OCTOBER

SECTION	BUSINESS TYPE	LICENSE AMOUNT	FEE	PENALTY	CITATION	INTEREST	TOTAL
081	COMMISSION MERCHANT OR MERCHANDISE BROKER	37.50	1.00	0.00	0.00	0.00	38.50

TRANSFER OF LICENSE
Evidence having been adduced before me that a bona fide sale of the business licensed by this certificate has been made by licensee, this license is transferred to said purchaser.

_____
Name of Purchaser
Issuing Authority

THOMAS L WHITE JR
State Comptroller

JULIE P. MAGEE
Commissioner of Revenue

REESE McKINNEY, JR.
Issuing Authority

TOTAL	38.50
MAIL FEE	0.00
TOTAL WITH MAIL FEE	38.50

L3 11/08/2011 11:42AM CASH

11/08/2011 11:42AM
PLANET IMAGINATION JCNS VIDEO MUSIC
& STORY PUBLISHING
1242 SETH JOHNSON DRIVE
MONTGOMERY AL36116
081 - COMMISSION MERCHANT OR
MERCHANDISE BROKER 38.50
Total: 38.50

Acct Number 030120

License#: 0003945

www.ingramcontent.com/pod-product-compliance
Lightning Source LLC
Chambersburg PA
CBHW040057160426
43192CB00002B/92